THIS *insatiable* AUGUST

THIS *insatiable* AUGUST

poems by
MAUREEN CLARK

Signature Books | 2024 | Salt Lake City

For Jon with love
and for my parents Jim and Blanche Record

Join our mail list at www.signaturebooks.com for details on events and related titles we think you'll enjoy.

Design by Jason Francis

FIRST EDITION | 2024

Paperback ISBN: 978-1-56085-473-9
Ebook ISBN: 978-1-56085-491-3

CONTENTS

THIN HYMN

SURFACING

Acknowledgments

My gratitude to the following journals in which the poems first appeared:

Alaska Quarterly: Lavender Dress
Bellingham Review: Getting it Wrong; As it Turns Out; Surfacing; Routine; On the Verge (B-Flat Fridge)
City Art Journal: Circumstance; As Though Gravity
Colorado Review: Sunday Song; Variable Moon
Dialogue: A Journal of Mormon Thought: Breach Birth: Aug. 20, 1891; Delineation; Utah Territory, 1893
Gettysburg Review: Premature Autopsy
Hawai'i Pacific Review: Fit of the Spoon
Irreantum: Between the Gods; Curious Tree
Lumina: It Comes to Nothing
Main Street Rag: Joshua Trees
Puerto del Sol: Two-Way Radio
Prairie Schooner: Killing Turkeys
Salt Flats Annual: Articulation; Root Cellar; Sestina for Edith
Southeast Review: Most of All a Future
Spoon River Poetry Review: Thin Hymn
Sugarhouse Review: Breath
Tar River Poetry: Degrees of Motion
Torrey House Press: Acrostic Lifeboat; Aquamarine
Utah Sings: Used Eclipse; In Every Nook
Willow Springs Magazine: Psalms 1–4

My gratitude to the following writers for their support and influence: Katharine Coles, Peggy Shumaker, David Lee, Shahid Ali, Jacqueline Osherow, David Revell, Brenda Miller, Jeff Metcalf, Lisa Linsalata and Dawn Marano.

Sunday Song

I.

I am an ill-formed garment,
congregation of one
sewing oil into water.

II.

Wind is worrying something into shape.
Is it a boat or an axe?

III.

Put your left-hand
under my head
just
above water
where I can smell
apples.

AS IT TURNS OUT

Most of All a Future

I won't go to a heaven without sagebrush or mosquito bites or thistle itch.
What's the point of paradise without orange - sections and sunsets?
Or the sting of salt water in microscopic cuts, the smell of ocean?

I'm not going if there's no sex. And not that metaphorical sex
you read about in poems. Real orgasmic sex.
Marimba, salsa, umbrella-opening sex. Miracle

Sex. Slow-sonata, candelabra sex.
And oracles like those of comets and zinnias,
yeast and elephants, the wrinkles on a cheek.

How perfect that zippers travel in only two directions,
a zigzag in the framework of story. Anticipation!
What can recommend mortality except the bite of winter

and the sweet return of birdsong, a letter arriving from a future tense?
I want the splinter so it can be removed. And gloom.
I want all the green at once, memories of imagined lovers and loss.

Some say the body is a residence for the soul, but I think the body is Braille
for the earthbound, a primer so we can touch our way towards death.
I know you in starlight and sun, with and without clothes.

When I become bone, I need to know the long slim commas of your ribs.
I can't explain this kind of dementia. Is the heart the first thing to go?
Will it be alchemy becoming fine as face powder? When I lose weight, finally,

I want a paradise somewhere of sex and imperfection
with a past and a present, but most of all a future.

Ordinary Mouths

Night breeze like a tenor sax plays a solo
through the catalpa leaves.

Deer forage through the backyard.
What is it about a long marriage?

You've been gone fourteen hours and
already I'm wearing your denim shirt.

A mathematician would construct
a story problem of us:

Two lovers leave a train station
traveling in opposite directions,

with a gauntlet for the left hand.
How long before they meet again

and grin like those two fools
in the wedding photograph,

who looked into the future
with such artless naïveté?

Autumn trees leave y's and v's
making umlauts of sky.

Mountains a jumble of colors
we can taste with our ordinary mouths.

circumstance

for Jon

It wouldn't happen all at once, like falling
in love—the unfettered tumble
of sense for sensuality, flinging

clothes and caution to the floor—the gamble
we started with—absolutely blind,
just like the old saying. We were all fumble

and buttons, rush and push, the bluster
and static of touch. I have adored you
through the ache and burn

of circumstance. I have followed
you through this fascination with light and sound
and watched me turn to hollow

delights my attention so easily found,
captured by a stray word, aware
of being nabbed again, drowned,

unable to stop the pull of language. Still, I dare
to praise that blue moon under which I found you.
How could I unknot the intricate tatting of what we share

undo the web of finely woven rituals of our youth,
the tiny knots we made to hold, to last.
Lace hardens with each passing year

brittle as slivers of glass.
When removed from you I will calcify,
become rheumatic, wither like witch grass

to a permanent winter, dry
into a spiked hedge, impenetrably charmed
with black magic—petrified

for a hundred years with no happily ever after to mourn,
because I've already been there. Yours is the only death
that would turn me entirely thorn.

Variable Moon

The best muses are unattainable.
—Iris Murdoch

I look for you
in the usual places.

Under stones
and twigs,

between the wings
of gypsy moths,

in the mulch
and on the wind.

I look for you
over the moon's

arched back,
and inside

my own reflection
in mirrors.

And I find you
in each chamber

of honeycomb,
every ibis feather.

I want to own
some relic of you,

a lock of hair,
perhaps an eyelash

you don't need
anymore.

Some small talisman
that carries your face.

Which is the last thing
I really need.

You're everywhere
already.

And I am a little
like the sun,

a magnet pulling,
wanting you

just so.
Waiting for you

I dream of
interesting teeth

and the lip's crooked tilt
into smile,

a palm
cushioning the chin,

and the smooth
nape of your neck.

What are the names
you answer to?

And the ones
you never had?

I will call you
Edith or Anne

Judith or Esther,
the names of my aunts.

They were tall
and beautiful.

Four sisters
nothing like me,

but I'm fond of their names.
I'll give you one.

Have you been
waiting long?

I'm not Laura
or the dark lady.

What name
will you give me?

I am no one's muse,
for which I am not grateful!

Would you call me Jerusha
or Hester?

Call it a fit of distraction
this gazing into ponds

searching for the right look,
the come-hither.

This must be how
the looking glass turns

inside-out.
The surface ripples and some familiar

gesture shifts and shimmers
double-chin, creases and lines.

What if age
were beautiful?

We are both
someone's daughter.

When the stars blur,
will you be my variable moon?

If I could say anything to you,
I'd say pomegranate,

sapphire, tornado, iris.
I'd say,

you are all these things
and more,

the little o-shaped
seeds, the tempest's eye

and the flutes of blossoms,
throats, curved earlobes,

the pockets of the pomegranate
holding the musey things

you feed to me,
one seed at a time.

And when I look in the mirror
it is you who turns.

I recognize the light
on your cheek, the coy lift

of your right shoulder.
If I could say anything, I'd say

Fairybell
Bitterroot

Monkeyflower
Speedwell

In Every Nook

Black umbrellas
hold their skirts down
even when there's no wind.
Trying to shut the giddy conduit
between what is said and what is heard,
fact or fiction, news, nostalgia.

Black umbrellas close in upon themselves.
The plaza is empty because it's winter,
but it doesn't matter.
In every nook there is passion
for the first time, heart-over-head
with leather, or the buttons on a shirt.

Black umbrellas like fat fence posts
make long shadows for secret meetings.
Things move us without permission
and language is the worst offender,
unhooking the shut places,
bewildering the hem of things.

Island

Night insects clicking.
Aspen leaves clacking.

He is a quiet island.
Listen to the movement of jackrabbits

and brine flies, the spaces between.
The ear is an erotic instrument.

He is the master of negative capability.
Maybe that's why this marriage works

most of the time. We fill the gaps
in each other's silence.

Salt grass and sand rub together.
It's almost too much of nothing.

Getting it Wrong

Imagine Vesalius in his room with the pilfered body of a woman
recently dead. She is cold and rubbery, in good condition,
a rare find, this woman with her inferior anatomy.
When he peels back the skin, he exposes her

cold insides. Her skin is rubbery
to his touch. The fluids run
when he peels back the skin and exposes her
muscles to the candlelight, the bright knife

touching her. His hands swim in the messy fluids
mapping her interior places,
muscles in candlelight, the bright knife
glistering in the body's envelope.

Mapping this interior space is messy,
so many little nerves to pull out
of the body's glistering envelope. The open
cabinet of the chest, the secret hollow of the abdomen,

where little tendons hold the mysterious organ
in place. He labels all the rivers braiding
her chest and abdomen. In the deep hollow
he finds her wandering organ, the fist-sized toad.

He labels the nerves that braid her like rivers,
like currents. The womb is a tiny planet in a bloody sky,
a hop toad, tadpole, croaking toad, wanderer.
This organ of woman's magic, hysteria, melancholy, desire.

The womb is dark and full of shooting stars.
Vesalius is in the universe under his hands,
the birthplace of magic, melancholy, hysteria,
desire, that only he has touched. How the charting

blinded him, a whole universe under his hands
in good condition, cold, the body of a woman
open, touched. His careful chart
getting it all wrong, this woman with her inferior anatomy.

Premature Autopsy

I.

My hands will be warm
when they enter your body
cutting through skin
and layers of muscle

to find the ghostly pleura
wrapped around your heart.
I will lift each lung
heavy as a premature baby

all yellow-pink, cradle in my palms
your four-chambered heart,
each semi-lunar valve, stilled.
The barbs are the best part of you.

Even in this soft place I am pierced.
I thread the branches of your arteries
leaving small prints like petals
of heartsease, here and there.

II.

The visible man can only
be reassembled one way,
otherwise, some parts
will have to be left out.

III.

How can I hear you
if your throat is a dry riverbed?
Your body in my hands
is a cello, an oboe,

an illuminated text.
My busy fingers
are counting your exquisite ribs.
I am an amateur.

Who said *dream not of other worlds*?
Inside your brain there is
a tree of life, a canopy of nerves
the skeleton of a skylark.

The stitches on your bound edge
will be neat and regular. I will chart
the galaxies of your freckles
and swallow the paper on which they are written.

Articulation

I.

One bone at a time: femur, tibia, mandible,
little bags of metatarsals and vertebrae.
Don't be alarmed!
The skeleton is a scaffold, teeth are jewels.
Can you imagine less devotion?
I rub the breaches between your bones
until I have memorized their geometry,
until I can articulate you with my eyes closed.

II.

It begins with the hand,
even in death a promise
of embrace
the way the thumb
curves to kiss the palm.

III.

If I washed your feet just once,
I'd remember the arch of your sole,
your heel cupped in my hands,
water, my head bent low,
how I am betrayed.

Root Cellar

O to be layered
cool and dark and full of onions.

I long to remove things
one filmy layer at a time, and sir

you don't help, being who you are.
Roots seek water and crevice,

convert rocks to their purposes,
which are and are not, binding.

The roof of your mouth is
more desired than honey.

Your words go down sweet and sticky.
The lips of those who sleep, sing.

On the packed dirt floor
barrels of apples and onions,

carrots and potatoes.
I am never prepared enough for winter.

One Note

In Debussy's
Girl with the Flaxen Hair
(near the end)

lifts me clean off the earth
holds me suspended
just long enough

that I think I understand
how sorry birds are
that we have arms.

Mornings among
the strings of patio lights
and lawn furniture

I break through invisible webs
from the tiniest spiders.
But O, remembering that one note

is redemption.
I'm pinned to the stars briefly
flung back along the arc of my body.

Aquamarine

Been a fool too many times:
obsession with a beam of light,
spoken words, something separate

but more than itself,
like aquamarine. Underwater,
how that color wavers

between blue and green
undulates into dream.
I unfold willingly,

a little bit at a time.
I unfold all at once,
a bolt of fabric flung.

Attracted to eyebrows arching
spaces between teeth,
teeth overlapping teeth, the mouth itself.

Flooded with thirst for men I hardly know
and women's faces. I can't stop being moved
by words spoken, light seduction.

As it Turns Out

These words will embarrass you in public,
    but you will understand them.
Two dragonflies' mate in mid-air.

So, is it just adoration? Obsession?
    Cosmic bowling?
You could be anyone as it turns out.

I needed someone to worship.
    You came along in the nick of time.
The weeds are thin out there.

You could bolt at any moment,
    a pheasant in October brush.
I can't conjure indifference.

I'm coming towards you with my palms up.
    If I'm lucky you won't run,
or move towards me.

Take this library full of books,
    erase all the words in them.
This is how it feels to write it down.

TWO-WAY RADIO

Lavender Dress

The path up and down is one and the same.
—Heraclitus

It would be interesting to do it all backwards,
start out old and grow young,
the arthritic knuckles bending like fabric
instead of wood, cataracts clearing
before your very eyes.

Imagine the startling climax, foreplay after.
Following looks. Remorse before the sin. Temptation
a dangling leftover.   Breasts fade
into the slim girl-body.
To know starting out that the boy

you wait for at the 9th Grade dance
has already stood you up,
no matter how many times
you lean against the tiled wall
of the gymnasium.

And still, you will go out
and buy the lavender dress.

Degrees of Motion

The cherry tree blossoms in a single day
buds of iris on the verge   ready to unfold.
Crumbling bricks are full of bees
busy with the pollination of fruit.
Wings hum under the porch eaves, small machines
motors   gears, the machinations of the century.

What will I know by the end of the century?
How bees find the hive at the end of the day
the secret language of machines
the illusion of control? Cherry blossoms unfold,
the hard nut gathers   and creates the fruit
around itself   reddens   calls to the male worker bees

and those females nudged in the head by the mother bee
to inhibit the growth of their ovaries. For centuries
my family has lived on this continent   *the fruited*
plains   you know the story   and how you need a day
when the story changes direction. Cerebral cortex folds
increases   folds again with language into a new machine.

This brain   the bee's patterns of flight   the washing machine
knocking unbalanced in the basement. The bees'
dance   waggle   repeat their flight   the folds
of the map they have drawn for centuries
the flowers are here   and here   a day's
journey and you can have it all   all the fruit

in the orchard.   Cherry trees are full of fruit
with their pits geared like tiny machines.
How long is a century   or a day?
Split open this cherry   and see the brain the bees
have made.   They've been working for centuries
nudging pollen onto their legs and bellies   the folds

of their wings strong and dropping pollen into unfolding
petals. The question is   how does the fruit
call from the blossom   like a thought over the centuries
this is what I will become?   The machine
is already at work. Hear the motors the bees
are turning   hear the work of another day.

The next century will unfold like a machine
made of   bees and blossoms   each day
heavy with fruit and stones.

Breach Birth: 20 Aug 1891

We are not teaching polygamy or plural marriage, nor permitting any person to enter into its practice.
—Wilford Woodruff, President
The Church of Jesus Christ of Latter-day Saints
October 6, 1890

Grandfather was born breach—meaning gap,
so that from the beginning
he was negative space,
a blue cast shadow,
a blur in the background,
a squint in his father's eye,

on the cusp of the proclamation to end polygamy,
in the Utah Territory, Swede Town,
in this very house
where his mother labors.

He was an unstitched seam
between blood and water,
a dangling thread not quite cast off,
draggling in dirt between his fathers'
religion and his pocketbook,
two unreachable shores.

Luck would be his religion.
He lived with that arbitrary grace.
He was a shadow on the porch,
a blank face under the brim of a hat,
a thread of light along the jaw.

Utah Territory, 1893

A washed cup
folded socks

three unworn shirts
with no scent of him

smooth bedsheets
dry towels.

She begins to know
something of scapegoats

left to wander unburned.
This promised desert

is not a rose at all
whose white petals fall

counted. All the grasses
are in Nebraska

blowing westward
in golden waves.

Near the un-mended fence,
an empty barn,

two children quick as sparrows
in the dirt-packed yard.

Delineation

I. 1971:

October snow brought the hunters
down from the mountains
without their kill. Sometimes
it happens this way.
Sumac and Oak were still clothed in red
burdened with snow   their trunks
splitting open   damp wood.
Power lines down
across the valley,
a perfect stage for his departure.

II. Inventory:

four pairs of brown pants
old man suspenders
a brace of shirts
garden gloves caked with earth
1946 Pontiac, maroon
a rocking chair of wood
six old radiators
the house in Swede Town.

III. Photograph:

He is third from the left, back row
between Otto and Harry,

boys from the neighborhood.
Someone has written 1916 – Swede Town

in blue ink on the back. Maybe it's spring,
hard to tell if the snow is almost melted

or almost enough. The angle of the camera
has captured his shadow, just above his right shoulder.

IV. Story:

This is the rocking chair
he was sitting in
when the Feds
raided the house
looking for the whisky,
that was hidden
under the floorboards,
under the braid rug,
under this particular chair,
where he sat rocking
my infant mother.

Two-Way Radio

After they took her to the hospital, my father took off his gun,
put an apron over the blue-black uniform,
and mopped the floor while I copied my spelling words

at the kitchen table. He burned the soup
and ironed crescent moons into his shirts.
Every morning my braids were a riddle for him,

the way the church women were for me
how they itched to call me motherless.
Winter fog settled in the valley like the mounds

of dirty laundry in the basement, making
every street a foreign country.
In the kitchen, my father chopped onions

each layer a pocket, a two-way radio.
In bed at night, I used to hear their voices
through the wall, the small endearments

so that when I learned to speak
I called her *honey* and *sweetheart.*
He took me to see her after two weeks

when the doctors said she was out of the woods
as though the stopping of her heart
had taken her to some other country and back.

Constellations

I.

My father dredged a river more than once
for the missing, presumed drowned.

In the newspaper photograph
he leans the pole into the gray water

to bring up the body and the red tricycle
two dark stars to the surface.

II.

An astronomy lesson of sorts,
my father's freckled constellations

on the backs of my hands.
Explain why my father looks back at me

from the mirror each morning as
I surface through the lake of glass.

III.

Each year the Farmer's Almanac
shows the phases of the moon,

the best time for planting corn.
Elderberries bud in their own good time,

clusters of purple and somehow my father knows
on which morning they will be ripe.

Killing Turkeys

for my father

I.

He gets up early
puts on the gold coveralls,

the garden boots,
and his Intermountain Farmers cap.

He's been fighting with the turkeys
since spring,

tossing them off the roof of the coop
again and again, and again.

We can tell it's started when we hear
damn stupid birds.

Mom drops the bread pans,
closes the drapes,

sends us to the basement
to watch cartoons.

My sister refuses to be pacified with Tom
and Jerry and says

she won't eat on Thanksgiving.
She cries until she has a stomachache.

II.

He comes in the back door
pale and bloody.

His hands shake as he washes the knife.
Does he remember

the hit and run as he rinses
the blood from his arms

the two-year-old dead
before he and his partner arrived

and called for backup?
Or the boy who wrapped

the stolen car around a tree;
blood freckling the windshield

and the sycamore.
I don't know what he has seen

through the blood-stippled glasses
he holds under the faucet.

When he is my father again
he is barefoot and clean,

watching the Padres
take on the Cardinals.

Up in Spirals

Something long buried is pushing up
from Mount Olivet Cemetery,
where the dead have long returned to dust.

November won't close up with snow.
Losses multiply. I drive the narrow streets between
the headstones. All that's left of a life,

a few numbers, an arrangement of letters.
Does it matter in the end,
what force animates the dead leaves?

Where it comes from and where it goes?
The weightless leaves
settle back into the gutters

utterly worn out
with the frantic thing
that looked like living.

Little Altars

Red poppies tilt
in the frame
like blowsy windmills

leaning eastward
toward the room
where the man

sleeps off the chemo.
In the indigo bowl
thin bits of shell

like broken bread.
Four tiny orange peppers
on a white plate,

dried and delicate
as tissue paper.
A lop-sided heart

of pink sandstone.
They will be here in the morning
these little altars.

Whatever needed
doing is already done.
The red poppies whisper sleep,

the orange peppers hang
like Chinese lanterns
in the bowl of night.

As Though Gravity

for Joe and Lisa

The mattress remembers your shape.
Deep hip and shoulder grooves show the hull of your body.
The feather pillow keeps

the impression of your head, as though gravity
still has hold of you, as if the shelter
of your body were just there instead of this muddy

divide between here and that winter.
How long before I understand the order of loss?
Wind drones like a chanter practicing

quavers. Aromas fade from your clothes,
the chairs. Memory slips the traces of flung
light. I can only taste your mouth

dreaming of you, restless in my sleep.
Lace-winged insects the color of peridot
and fog, play a rhapsody

so fragile, a cough might
shatter it into nothing but empty air.
I wake up alone, the form of you just there.

Sestina for Edith

The children have chosen the word: *apricot*
from the big envelope. They are writing sestinas. Now the word: *burn.*
They squirm in their seats for the next word.
Grandma Edith stirs the jam with a wooden spoon.
Next, they choose *gate.*
The thick smell of fruit brings back her ghost.

The children want ghosts
to be scary, not my grandmother, and not apricots.
But I am a child suddenly and the gate
is open. What can you do with six words if you have to burn
in every stanza? *Come and lick the spoon*
Grandma pantomimes from the window. The important word

is any word since the stroke. We talk without words,
the way we always did, like mirrored ghosts
stirring the hot syrup with her spoon.
This was before I knew that apricots
came from Arabia, before I burned
jam in the kitchen in Fargo, setting off the smoke alarm. The gate

is open. I spent hours swinging back and forth on the gate
between my house and Grandma's. I give her all my words,
but it doesn't help. Her ability to speak has burned
away, but she is not a ghost
yet. I bring her apricots.
We dip them in the hot water one by one, with a round spoon

just the right size, a slotted spoon,
so we can lift them out quick, peel off their skins. I can hear gates
opening among the children. Apricot
with its three even syllables is a magic word
now, and I am my grandmother's ghost,
braiding a story from nothing. Edith burns

trying to speak my name. See her freckles burned
into the backs of my hands? We take up the spoon
to stir the jam. Ritual brings out her ghost.
The children are little gates
opening. They choose six words
from the envelope. I smell apricots.

Edith is at the gate beckoning me with a spoon.
The children write quick with their six words.
The room is burning, full of apricots and ghosts.

Breath

When you die—well, you go with your
Last breath and find the others.
—William Stafford

Between bough and crown,
where the last breath

meets up with all the others;
under leaf and needle, moisture

hangs on the fibers of a web.
Birds darn the canopy, skim

from bush to loom a sky made
entirely of dip and dance.

Crows gather strands of clothing.
The white moon skates across the coming night,

trailing that last exhalation,
that floss of air.

Routine

Trust the pores of your skin,
the smell of bread and oranges.

This is not a manifestation,
no mist among tombstones.

The dead are already tethered here
by routine. Stir the soup.

What's the worst that could happen?
Fold a shirt. Make the bed.

This is no will-o-wisp come to catch.
No fairy circle. Do an ordinary task.

Knead the bread. Sugar the tea.
See how he rolls a cigarette,

my dead grandfather?
He licks the edge of the paper

and twists the ends.
Smell the sulfur of the match.

The red glow, there, across the room.
Until morning, trust in that.

THIN HYMN

It Comes to Nothing

Waiting for God or elephants
memory of laughter wanders the empty yard

with the smell of ripe peaches.
Rescuers twist through the high Rocky's

searching for the lost boy,
or the glove of his body.

Right now, a wasp
walks on the boy's delicate eyelid.

The grass around him moves like a skirt.
All those ripe peaches will go unplucked.

Perhaps the boy is looking for spaces
in the fence, or dolphins in the meadow

decorated with flags. This insatiable August
cleaves to the rescuer's bodies.

Their losses laid out like feathers.

Psalm 1

Can you hear me
among the sycamores?
Just a two-note complaint

on the dark carpet of this pasture.
Crickets saw the legs off night
leaving shadows thin as onion skin,

spare as the pages of dawn
the east is waiting to turn.
Can you hear me?

My incessant complaints,
my curses in their predictable gowns,
cloth already limp and shiny

at the elbows and knees.
Even the horses
do not acknowledge me.

Field mice and beetles
keep their appointments.
They will not lift their heads

to this place where I stand
exposing my ugly wings,
throwing my voice up again and again.

Spliced

Envelopes were empty, their letters flown.
Inside peaches, hard stones.

Under soil, perfectly formed hyacinth bulbs.
Inside thunderheads roiling storms, floods.

Waves brought the flotsam I rubbished through.
My life, a movie I'd seen too many times, though

I knew exactly where the celluloid would break,
spliced right there with a razor blade and sticky tape.

Used Eclipse

Between the million names for God
a shepherd moon circles the far

ring of Saturn, while
bison on Antelope Island lift their heads

to the gang of seagulls in the parking lot
fighting for trash. Rabbit brush

and salt grass whisper
while the buffalo sing

at the watering hole.
Those huge bodies, strange

in the peculiar light
of this used eclipse.

Between what is sacred
and Sunday, October

comes and the mazy veins
of morning-glory

in the pasture
dry out and let go.

Psalm 2

Tree shadows grow down the wall. Late afternoon sun
lengthens the trunks into thin toothpicks.

They cannot stay still. Shadows
move the slat fence across my face.

Leaves stretch downward
darkness strumming their contours.

I would scrape my insides out for an answer,
hollow these limbs for flight,

but, my arms are heavy with marrow.
My feet carry my burdens with me

into the next room, where leaf shadows
grow long, down longer walls.

Curious Tree

The branches of trees
like curious arteries
of some invisible God

go willy-nilly in all directions.
Sight defines reality
the tangerine peel empty

fitted back together. Bound by dust
the mystics yearned
for permeable boundaries,

not prophecy and order,
a spirituality
that sight could pass through.

Hope slips away from me
over the edge of the round earth.
Some mornings it rises again,

some mornings
it stays in Australia.
Whatever phase the moon is in,

it will return, keep its promise.
Perhaps you should buy three bags
of fortune cookies for a dollar,

everything being equal.
God, if both of us are lost,
which one of us will lead?

Comparison

To whom will ye like me . . . that we may be like?
—Isaiah 46:5

Would it be voltage or vortex
or is that too scientific?
Every simile needs a body.

Heaven is half a memory
from a Sunday School lesson,
a tune caught in my mind,

notes drifting off, lost again.
That ditty that gets caught
in the ear like a gnat

humming under the lobe
unreliable as angels.
I can't remember the words.

What is the crux of the metaphor?
The question is 'to whom'
and I don't have an answer.

Maybe the best I can do
is find an understudy.
I'll keep knocking,

but it's all a ruse.
There is no comparison.
Why would anyone

dare be a simile for God?
Is there an equal sign for deity?
Here in the west

miracles are expected
in crickets and seagulls
rain and sego lilies.

Still there is no likeness.
Not even tools as tangible
as stained-glass

in the colors of hallelujah are enough.
I should ask God
who he would compare to me

but the line is busy.
It's a trick question anyway,
one that needs a Canterbury

a redemption by hoodoo
pincushion cactus
something dirt red, something said.

Naked Bulb

I.

Do you want me pressed and perfect
or come as you are?

Bend me towards a shore.
Let shoes be optional.

If I were a moth
I'd navigate by the stars.

Nature is out of control:
a curse, a blessing, a corporeal thing.

Listen, is that the hum of electricity
or God speaking with the voices of insects?

II.

The hawk is drawn to the heartbeat of the mouse,
moths like addicts to a needle fling themselves

against the naked bulb and become sparks,
the smell of blood and metal

instinct causing wings to beat too close to the light.
Lunar dust spills across an inky heaven.

III.

Burn them at the margins
As they flit into the halo of light

becoming one with the ardent dark
around your ultimate spark

where you with nonchalance
torch another worshiper.

IV.

I once thought I had you
all wrapped up, and then I didn't.

My garden is crawling with fresh
blue morning glory and bindweed.

Let's just say this God,
the porch-light moon fools the moths and me.

Acrostic Lifeboat

Take words with you and return to God.
—Hosea 14:3

The bug zapper flashes Morse code,
A spark for each dot and dash - saying - pay attention. Words are being
Kindled from these fried insects. The rise and fall of empires depend on
Each death. Our elliptical orbit brings another year of language.

Why would you take words to return to God? Why not bundles of wheat?
Oil in clay jars? Fresh baked bread. Why not take salt?
Red wine, purple cloth, things more like worship?
Depending on the alphabet is risky with its creation of ambiguity
Scratched onto vellum, painted on papyrus, so much lost in translation. Poems

Written on napkins and grocery receipts.
I can't deny that I'm compelled, enticed even,
To thrust my fingers into a bowl of letters and return
Holding on for dear life, writing 'lifeboat' just in time,

Yielding to the possible safety of the right word.
Only language can tell our stories. Some letters generate echoes of the
Utterly haunting past, mistakes, the resonance of the earth.

Any word can be a talisman. I've always wanted to
Nail down how civilization evolved into writing. I want to write the word
Dromedary because the cadence mirrors the way it moves.

Ridiculous of course, but I'd ride that one-hump camel to the oasis any day.
Even the unvoiced desire can eventually be put into words, and spells
To cure warts, whip up a tempest, make a magic potion.
Unless words carry different weights like numbers and can be
Rounded up or down. Someone show me the runes!
Never mind, I've wandered off again,

Too full of questions that can't be answered
Overwhelmed with finding a word to rhyme with orange,

Grappling with the alphabet, the number of syllables in a perfect line,
One too many or needing one less. It's futile. Please take my words God,
Do whatever it takes to return to me.

Milk

I.

I'd know what to expect
from a God who loved me. Wouldn't I?

The road out of religion
filled me with terrible angels.

My soul worth
no more than a gallon of milk

on the kitchen floor.
Too much to wipe up.

II.

Go to the lake and hold still.
Smell the brine

the decomposing plants.
Pad across oolitic sand

enter into the salty water.
Let it hold you like a baby.

III.

Bison trample the sagebrush.
What can I believe now?

A blue heron rises from the cattails.
This is what I know:

when I take my last breath
I want a shore to be there, a slap of water

against my boat, relief as tender
as my grandmother's hands.

Holes

Please, someone fill this God-shaped hole in me.
Nibbled crumbs fall now that I'm good and empty.

Take my whitest hairs, threads of cloth from this dark loss.
Build a nest. I always wanted to be useful.

Make music. Cover the holes in me with your fingers.
Let the glass flute of my skin make the keening sound of a far-off ship.

Let the reeds of my bones play a song of sorrow.
Blow air across me, beyond me. Now that I am empty,

measure the cups of star dust I am made from.
Please, craft a bucket from my chest.

Now that I'm empty, pray to the six directions.
Hold me open and give shape to this grief.

Thin Hymn

At the year's end,
when the dry leaves smell of spent lives,
and all the lives are mine.

This year of small deaths
and gone days,
my mouth full of dead words.

Can the rain come?
Can it come now in a flood rush?
In the last hour,

can it come soon in a mud gush?
Can the dry leaves of this scorched year
make a small book,

a thin hymn to failed faith
and hushed hope,
gone friends and deep hurts?

Just a brief rain
and the wraiths gone
from the heart's shore

a slow boat
to the far bank of the wide night.
Let the hush come.

SURFACING

Joshua Trees

Take the long way around
on the way to Vegas.

Bypass the Virgin River Gorge
and stop inside this national forest

where the trees look more like yucca plants and
this wet spring gave them each a tight bundle

of yellow blossoms at the tip of each branch.
These far-spaced trees are a secret of the Mojave.

No taller than a man or woman
they are placed like goal posts

in acres of sage and sand.
They won't offer you a pencil of shade,

and yet, there is a protection here
those rows of perfect apple trees

and dizzy fields of lavender can't match.
You can finally let go.

The ancestors hold out
their short arms towards you.

Surfacing

for Janice

I.

The hammock rocks on its harness,
storm coming.

I am a baby
tossed into a swimming pool.
I can see it happen, but I have no language
to call for help. In nightmares water still rises in my mouth.

Prepositions matter
when the subject is water.

At swimming lessons, I go under
in the deep end, like falling
in slow motion. I am submerged so long
I pray for gills, give all my dolls to my sister.

Thunder breaks along the Wasatch,
comes back as echo.

I drown at the YMCA and pull my sister under with me,
for company. We take turns coming up for air.
We have always lived like this.

Rain comes down in drops too small
for drowning.

At thirteen I wanted to be
a flower that didn't grow in the desert:
Nymphaeales, water lily, floating cup.

I saw water lilies once at San Juan Capistrano,
there were bells ringing.

I try to drown at fourteen,
I have to know if water
will give me back.

II.

Cactus, yucca, woman,
evidence of things that survive drought.

Lake Powell exposes her trash:
tires, toilets, car batteries
beached on sandbars
beneath Fremont Indian cliff dwellings.
The sandstone notched for fingers and toes
thousands of years ago.

Slot canyons in Zion wash clean,
flashflood.

Rainbow Bridge dissolves
from the inside, out,
loosening itself a grain at a time,
carried by gusts and gales into arch,
downstream, sand, sediment, scree.

Before the saints enter the Salt Lake Valley
they change sacramental wine to water.

Great Salt Lake,
America's dead sea is
three times more salty than the ocean.
Before a rainstorm the wind churns up
lake stench, the perpetual decay
of living matter,
things that break down.

> Living in the desert you learn to thicken your hide,
> ration tears, gather dew into subterranean pools.

III.

> I suffocate on Sundays
> drowning in the old covenants.

The dry homily pushes me under
into the blurry depths of mud and roots
where water lilies attach and rise
to blossom on the surface.

> Instead of one answer, I want many.
> My thirst is always one swallow ahead of me.

Women are not meant to surface where I live.
I begin undrowning myself
without anyone's permission.
Being mostly water, I can take any shape I choose.

> If the lake has enough salt.
> I will be unsinkable.

Knotted Wrack

I can see now that it was a winter for travel
although I never left the house in Bountiful
and the cat rarely traveled
far from the southern windowsill   I traveled
to the edge of belief   my religion   like seaweed
tangled around my ankles   pleading to some God: help me traverse
this trouble   the loss of the religion I traveled
with my whole life.   I am searching for the right word
to describe this battle with my old self   those unpredictable words
that I see out there beyond my small life.   I want to travel
to those exotic places where I might find the woman
I believe I really am   the woman

I want to be   authentic and unrepentant as thunder and lava   the woman
just out of my reach   the object of all my inner battles.
I have been defined: *weaker sex*   *helpmeet*   *the kept woman*
goodwife   *better half*   *one of nature's agreeable blunders*   *the woman*
behind the man   *sister*   *second-class citizen.* I live in the heart of Bountiful
where my story is full of women ruled by religion   women
sacrificed to religion   for man's love of God more than woman
the tangled sacred sense of God turns out to be the Devil's shoelace seaweed
in thin filaments that trip the logic   beached lumps of seaweed
the smell of salt   a time of wrack and loss and women
cast up   cast out   scapegoats.   I want a word
to describe this kind of wordlessness.

I am labeled   by language   so many words
none of them written   by women.
I am not a consolation prize   a word
that can be underlined   pinned down.   I am the word
dangerous   the word *wild.*   I can only travel
in one direction.   I'll be a scalpel cutting out the words
that insist I take someone else's word
for it   not my own   here in Bountiful.
I will weave an elaborate and bountiful
life of shells and string   and the words
I'm not supposed to think   question I can't ask   caught in this seaweed
my whole life   a sweet tangle of weeds

separating the self from the saint/sorceress/sinner/seaweed
the colors of the ocean I drown in.   I collect words
for kelp: knotted wrack   sea whistle   gulfweed
the cottage industry of green bottle seaweed
the metaphor for a woman's
hair   what is acceptable   what is not   chenille seaweed
black tang   lady wrack   carrageen
mermaid's fan.   I will find a way to travel
away from my past   unknotting myself   travel
to an ocean big enough for Saturn to float   surrounded by seaweed.
I will find answers there   that I can't find in Bountiful
where I drown in the unappreciated bounty

of identical houses   a cherry tree in each yard   a bountiful
place in this desert of salt   near the Great Salt Lake where no seaweed
beaches   just crusted salt   oolitic sand   the bounty
of silence   of being silent.   How ironic that Bountiful
is the place where I lose my religion   where it's just a word
for abundance   where I am finally full
of loss   enough   to let go   and accept the bountiful
imperfection of myself.   This is where I live   just a woman
who is naming herself   one letter at a time   a woman
who lives in a kind of poverty   so rich   I can be full
of questions.   My feet are bare.   I carry a jar of ointment.   I am a traveler
looking for answers.   I will choose what I need to take with me.   I travel

towards my own definition   the one I choose.
I travel alone into this bountiful place to become
a woman who gathers   words and stones.
shells and seaweed
a woman who hoards her verbs.

Psalm 3

Midday sun glimmers off the creek
scattering over rocks,

wildflowers, marsh.
Cottonwoods reach

roots into underground rivers,
unmoved by tempest,

flood or changing season.
Step into the mossy gravel.

Let gritty sand lodge between toes.
Track muddy footprints,

flatten the grass along the path
near the wild reeds.

The creek cold as liquid winter,
a word for ache. It's hard to look at

that brilliance arcing just there,
where the water rushes stones and

shouts, before crashing into more light.

The Fish and the Water Lily

Climbing out of the cave, forging tools as I go.
I've learned to jump, call out,

let someone hear me
from inside my jar.

I am the one thing that matters.
I am the fish and the water lily,

the papyrus and food.
My lid is off.

I'll yell until someone listens.
This is what I need:

a pail that carries water,
an axe for chopping wood,

flint arrowheads, a bow.
I wake every morning in pain

look for hawks in the sky,
the medicine that will heal me.

Fit of the Spoon

for Edith

I imagine my grandmother in her kitchen
with a grocery list on the table and the row of empty cans.

After the stroke she doesn't know the word for
cinnamon or *paprika* until she sees the letters

and copies them down. This is what she knows:
the fit of the spoon in her hand, the wide-mouthed canning jars,

wooden spoon, a tin funnel. She names things by touch
onion, tomato, both round, one makes you cry.

There she is by the Hotpoint stove
in her sensible black shoes.

The kitchen is full of spice.
She holds the infant me

as though I am the word she remembers.

Psalm 4

Since I cannot carry a tune, I will sing
with the voices of sycamore, raindrops, geraniums,
the meadowlark perched on a headstone,
the graves themselves singing aloud.

Join voices with comets
and constellations on the black sidewalk
of the firmament. Exult with hills,
meadows, sandstone bluffs, dawn coming up,
chains of scattered light, like a laugh.

All creation cries out together.
This wild hymn.

Open Window

Sweet honeysuckle
through an open window.
Sometimes grandma sings

about birds
and holding a sparrow
in her hand,

feeling the warm heart
beat against her palm.
She sings of everyday magic

how we all passed through
the bones of our mothers,
unharmed.

Come In

Among sun-leeched bones, the skulls
of animals in grit the color of sunset,
and soft as face powder under my feet.

The acute stillness rings without sound,
like a bruise slowly purpling under skin,
a dervish about to fly to pieces,

smooth velvet shade under
yellow willows, Earth so parched I can hear
the wind weave between the cactus, juniper and sage.

All it takes is a slight movement of air
to bring me to my knees
as though someone is listening.

On the Verge

Like birdsong beginning inside the egg.
—Rumi

My old skin has shriveled and gone.
I prefer ambiguity and displacement.

I hear that soft hiss coming from the orange juice
left out too long, the magic of fermentation.

Who knew there were so many sounds inside
cornstarch, plastic bags, seedpods, a cracker-box.

The b-flat fridge turns on in the kitchen.
Insects whir and click, music

of bare feet mooshing through sand.
It is what I can hear that truly exists.

On the verge of blue
I gave up expecting angels and

the universe broke open like an egg.

Messy Planet

Earth is so precisely blue in those NASA photographs,
so mud-brown close up. Yet, somehow,
it is the imperfect world I give my heart to

with all the sorrow locked in me like a root-bound tree.
I can't fathom my own skin replacing itself
or hope as literal as bone.

Sun flings light into oncoming traffic
across another Sunday morning.
What I know is a thin string of possibility.

Then the sudden smell of marzipan arrives
from my childhood, or last week
that lets the tree uproot a little, there at the fringe.

I can live with the dark ache of existence,
the violet crush of this messy planet. It's just that I want
to own one thing that's written down, a verse

that is pure purple, a plum hanging from a branch
like a jewel, a visible angel breaking the rules.
If there is a gate into that sun, let my grandmother guard it.